DEALING WITH TRUST ISSUES

Keys To Understanding and Solving Trust Issues

By

DAVID JOSEPH

All rights reserved. No part of this publication may be reproduced, distributed, or transmitted in any form or by any means, including photocopying, recording, or other electronic or mechanical methods, without the prior written permission of the publisher, except in the case of brief quotations embodied in critical reviews and certain other noncommercial uses permitted by copyright law. Copyright © (David Joseph), (2022).

Table of Content

Chapter 1

Chapter 2

Chapter 3

Chapter 4

Chapter 1

Trust

Trust is having faith that another person is trustworthy and sincere. It's how we erroneously assess another person's character, including their honesty and ability to uphold moral standards. However, there are instances when we are unsure about whom, when, or how much to trust. Trust is a personal indicator of how much we can rely on and have faith in the goodness and morality of others. However, we could experience trust challenges if our ability to believe in others is jeopardized.

Avoiding commitment in sexual relationships, avoiding deep friendships or social connections, and finding it difficult to forgive minor or incorrect slights are just a few of the symptoms of trust issues.

Negative childhood experiences, adult relationship infidelity, gaslighting, or narcissistic abuse from family members can all contribute to trust issues.

However, individuals can take personal measures to convey their uncertainty, be sensitive of their prior trauma, and be prepared to take the risk to overcome trust issues. Overcoming trust issues is best done with the support of a behavioral therapist or couples' counselor.

What exactly does Trust mean?

Prior to discussing how to restore trust, it is crucial to comprehend what trust actually is. To begin with, it can be beneficial to consider trust as a decision that someone must make. Someone cannot be made to trust you. Until someone proves they are deserving of your trust, you could decide not to provide it to them.

Signs of Trust in a relationship

Trust can mean different things to different people. In a romantic relationship, trust might mean:

- You feel committed to the relationship and to your partner.
- You feel safe with your partner and know they'll respect physical and emotional boundaries.
- You know your partner listens when you communicate your needs and feelings.
- You don't feel the need to hide things from your partner.
- You and your partner respect each other.
- You can be vulnerable together.
- You support each other.

It's crucial to comprehend what trust isn't.

For instance, trust in a relationship does not necessarily include telling your partner everything that comes to mind. To have private thoughts that you keep to yourself is very natural. Additionally, having mutual trust does not include access to:

- (Except if it's a shared account)
- computers, specifically
- mobile phones
- social networking sites

It's possible that you have no problem disclosing this information, especially in an emergency. However, having trust in a relationship typically means

Trust Issues

Trust issues are characterized by fear of betrayal, abandonment, or manipulation. And this fear is often triggered as a *result* of betrayal (such as infidelity), abandonment (think: leaving a child or foregoing a relationship with them), or manipulation (for example, dishonesty or gaslighting). If you're reading this, it's possible that someone you trusted — a partner, a parent, or even a doctor — mistreated you or let you down. And as a result, you struggle to trust others. Or, in other words, you have trust issues.

Many people can pinpoint the event or relationship in question, but others struggle. And most (if not all) struggle to overcome their trust issues.

However, it isn't impossible. If you're struggling with trust issues, you can work to trust again by following a few steps. But first, let's start from the beginning: What exactly *is* trust?

A healthy relationship must have trust, yet trust doesn't develop overnight. And once broken, it's hard to rebuild. Infidelity may be the first thing that comes to mind when you consider the situations that could make you lose faith in your partner. However, betraying someone's confidence in a relationship is not the only option.

Other possibilities include:
- a practice of breaking commitments or breaking your word, failing to support your spouse when they need you,
- withholding or holding anything back,
- lying, or manipulating
- a tendency to keep one's emotions to oneself

What Are Trust Issues and How Do You Know If You Have One?

Remember what we stated earlier? People who struggle with trust have a very hard time trusting people, frequently because someone has betrayed them in the past.

Here are additional signs and symptoms of trust issues:

- **They assume betrayal.** Those with trust issues assume someone has betrayed their trust even if they have no rightful reasoning.
- **They anticipate betrayal.** People with trust issues often assume someone will betray them soon enough, despite how honest they have been in the past.

- **They're overly protective.** Those with trust issues are usually very protective of their loved ones, out of fear that they will become disloyal.
- **They distance themselves from others.** People with trust issues decide it's best to limit their relationships to avoid betrayal or abandonment.
- **They avoid commitment.** No matter how much they care for someone, people with trust issues refuse to commit.
- **They refuse to forgive (even the smallest mistakes).** Those with trust issues are quick to make a big deal out of nothing — it's the end of the world if someone makes the slightest mistake.

- **They feel lonely or depressed.** Those with trust issues isolate themselves from others and feel lonely or depressed as a result.
- **They're excessively wary of people.** People with trust issues are extremely cautious and suspicious of everyone they meet.

What Causes Trust Issues?

We stated before that a betrayal, abandonment, or manipulating act is frequently the root of trust issues. But what are the most prevalent instances of these transgressions that cause trust problems?

- **Infidelity:** Once more, infidelity is a form of betrayal that can cause problems with trust.

This is often seen as the height of betrayal. While it is possible to mend a relationship after infidelity, this rarely happens since the victim of the infidelity ends up with trust difficulties that affect their ability to form healthy relationships in the future.

- **Manipulation or mistreatment:** You run a higher chance of developing trust issues if a former partner or loved one abused you. Examples include lying, gaslighting, acting passive-aggressively, and isolating you from other people.
- **Childhood Trauma:** Traumatic events as a child are also likely to lead to trust concerns. Adoption and abuse are two examples (by one or more caregivers).

- **Other types of Traumas**: Trust issues can also result from trauma experienced later in life. For instance, if you had a painful experience with a previous doctor, you might find it difficult to trust healthcare experts. Imagine receiving a false diagnosis for a critical condition.
- **Conflicts between parents:** If your parents are divorced, you may be more prone to having trust issues in general and in love relationships in particular. On the other hand, if your parents frequently quarreled and you saw their relationship fluctuate, you might have trouble trusting people.

When someone is betrayed, their trust issues may make it harder for them to prevent internalizing the incident; they may place the responsibility on themselves and become less self-assured moving forward.

This can affect their capacity for trust because they could feel "undeserving," and rather than creating a healthy connection, a person with trust issues may be always on guard, so to speak, waiting for the other shoe to drop.

Chapter 2

The Importance of Trust in Romantic Relationships

Whether they are the product of betrayal in a previous romantic engagement or not, our trust issues most often cause our romantic relationships to suffer. Why? Honesty and transparency are the cornerstones of intimate partnerships. The relationship is held together by the trust that the partners have in one another. This trust creates a strong emotional bond that is based in adoration, love, and loyalty. Infidelity is a frequent contributor to trust problems.

When one of the partners in a relationship cheats, the dishonesty and breach of trust may have a greater negative impact than the affair itself.

The partner has another area of their life that they've kept hidden, and lying undermines faith in the other person. A person will feel extra vulnerable to betrayal and deception by someone they loved if they did not learn to trust as a child.

Is Having Trust Issues a Mental Illness?

Having trust issues as a singular issue isn't a mental illness. However, it can be indicative of an actual mental health condition, particularly:

- Anxiety disorders, especially PTSD
- Borderline personality disorder (BPD)
- Paranoid personality disorder (PPD)
- Bipolar disorder I or II

These conditions may cause trust issues in relationships because of the way certain cognitive distortions, irrational beliefs, or mood swings may unrealistically change someone's perception of reality and interpersonal relationships. What can be particularly damaging, though, is when a person with a mental health condition that causes trust issues is hurt by a loved one's deception. This can affirm their negative bias and make it even harder to emotionally and socially connect with other people, even if they desire to do so.

What Is a Person Called When They Have Trust Issues?

Pistanthrophobia is the fear of trusting people or forming significant relationships with them.

While it's not a recognized mental health condition in the DSM-5, Pistanthrophobia, like other phobias, causes significant mental and emotional distress and usually detracts from the sufferer's quality of life in a significant way.

Are Trust Issues a Red Flag?

Trust issues can be a sign that someone has experienced a significant amount of trauma — but that doesn't mean that they aren't working through their past experiences. Trust issues in a relationship can be hard for both partners to overcome, but with adequate support and communication channels, people with trust issues can have healthy, successful connections with partners — that aren't ruled by their past.

What Do You Do If You Have Trust Issues in a Relationship?

Dialectical behavior therapy (DBT) is an effective treatment method for people who are noticing continued trust issues in relationships. So, for those wondering how to fix trust issues, finding a mental health professional that they can connect with and receive DBT from is the first place to begin. Partners can also benefit from couples or marriage counseling, where they'll learn new ways to empathize, communicate, and resolve differences and conflicts.

But even before beginning counseling or another form of mental health treatment, there are smaller, personal ways in which someone with trust issues in a relationship can begin to find healing.

How to Rebuild Trust After a Betrayal

- Defining trust
- If you've been betrayed
- If you've hurt someone
- Timeline
- Weighing your options
- Getting help
- Takeaway

Trust is an essential component of a strong relationship, but it doesn't happen quickly. And once it's broken, it's hard to rebuild.

When you think about circumstances that could lead you to lose trust in your partner, infidelity may come to mind right away. But cheating isn't the only way to break trust in a relationship.

Other possibilities include:

- a pattern of going back on your word or breaking promises
- not being there for your partner in a time of need
- withholding, or keeping something back
- lying or manipulation
- a pattern of not sharing feelings openly

What does trust really mean?

Before going over how to rebuild trust, it's important to understand what trust is, exactly.

To start, it might be helpful to think of trust as a choice that someone has to make. You can't make someone trust you. You might not choose to trust someone until they show that they're worthy of it.

Signs of trust in a relationship

Trust can mean different things to different people. In a romantic relationship, trust might mean:

- You feel committed to the relationship and to your partner.
- You feel safe with your partner and know they'll respect physical and emotional boundaries.
- You know your partner listens when you communicate your needs and feelings.
- You don't feel the need to hide things from your partner.
- You and your partner respect each other.
- You can be vulnerable together.
- You support each other.

It's also important to understand what trust *isn't*.

In a relationship, for example, trust doesn't necessarily mean you tell your partner every single thing that crosses your mind. It's totally normal to have personal thoughts you keep to yourself.

Trust also doesn't mean giving each other access to:

- bank accounts (unless it's a shared one)
- personal computers
- cell phones
- social media accounts

You may not mind sharing this information, especially in case of an emergency.

But the presence of trust in a relationship generally means you don't need to check up on your partner. You have faith in them and feel able to talk about any concerns you might have.

Chapter 3

Rebuilding trust when you've been betrayed

Having someone break your trust can leave you feeling hurt, shocked, and even physically sick. It might prompt you to consider your relationship — and your partner — in a different way. If you want to attempt to rebuild trust, here are some good starting points.

- **Consider the reason behind the lie or betrayal**

When you've been lied to, you might not care much about the reasons behind it. But people do sometimes lie when they simply don't know what else to do. This doesn't make their choice right, but it can help to consider how you might have reacted in their position.

Sure, your partner may have betrayed you to protect themselves, but they may have had a different motive. Were they trying to protect you from bad news? Make the best of a bad money situation? Help a family member?

Maybe the betrayal of trust resulted from a miscommunication or misunderstanding.

Whatever happened, it's important to make it clear that what they did wasn't OK. But knowing the reasons behind their actions may help you decide whether you're able to begin rebuilding the trust you once shared.

- **Communicate**

It might be painful or uncomfortable, but one of the biggest aspects of rebuilding trust after betrayal is talking to your partner about the situation.

Set aside some time to clearly tell them:
- how you feel about the situation
- why the betrayal of trust hurt you
- what you need from them to start rebuilding trust

Give them a chance to talk, but pay attention to their sincerity. Do they apologize and seem truly regretful? Or are they defensive and unwilling to own up to their betrayal?

You may feel emotional or upset during this conversation. These feelings are completely valid. If you feel yourself getting too upset to continue communicating in a productive way, take a break and come back to the topic later. Talking about what happened is just the beginning. It's perfectly fine, and entirely normal, if you can't work through everything in just a night or two.

- **Practice forgiveness**

If you want to repair a relationship after a betrayal, forgiveness is key. Not only will you need to forgive your partner, but you also may need to forgive yourself.

Blaming yourself in some way for what happened can keep you stuck in self-doubt. That can hurt the chances of your relationship's recovery. Depending on the betrayal, it might be hard to forgive your partner and move forward. But try to remember that forgiving your partner isn't saying that what they did was OK.

Rather, you're empowering yourself to come to terms with what happened and leave it in the past. You're also giving your partner a chance to learn and grow from their mistakes.

- **Avoid dwelling on the past**

Once you've fully discussed the betrayal, it's generally best to put the issue to bed. This means you don't want to bring it up in future arguments.

You'll also want to go easy on constantly checking in on your partner to make sure they aren't lying to you again. This isn't always easy, especially at first. You might have a hard time letting go of the betrayal and find it difficult to start trusting your partner, especially if you're worried about another betrayal.

But when you decide to give the relationship a second chance, you're also deciding to trust your partner again. Maybe you can't completely trust them right away, but you're implying you'll give trust a chance to regrow.

If you can't keep thinking about what happened or have misgivings about your partner's future honesty or faithfulness, couples counseling can help. But these signs could also indicate you may not be ready to work on the relationship.

Rebuilding trust when you've hurt someone

You messed up. Maybe you lied and hurt your partner or withheld information you thought would hurt them. No matter your reasons, you know you caused them pain, and you feel terrible. You may feel like you'd do anything to show them they can trust you again.

First, it's important to understand that the broken trust may be beyond repair. But if you both want to work on repairing the relationship, there are a few helpful steps you can take.

- **Consider why you did it**

Before you embark on the process of rebuilding trust, you'll first want to check in with yourself to understand why you did it.

Is it possible that you wanted to end the relationship but didn't know how to? Or were their specific needs that weren't being met by your partner? Or was it just a dumb mistake? Understanding the motives behind your behavior can be difficult, but it's a crucial part of rebuilding trust.

- **Apologize sincerely**

If you lied, cheated, or otherwise damaged your partner's faith in you, a genuine apology is a good way to start making amends. It's important to acknowledge you made a mistake.

Just remember that your apology isn't the time to justify your actions or explain the situation. If some factors did influence your actions, you can always share these with your partner *after* apologizing and owning your part in the situation.

- **Be specific**

When you apologize, be specific to show you know what you did was wrong. Use "I" statements. Avoid putting blame on your partner.
For example, instead of "I'm sorry I hurt you," try:

"I'm sorry I lied to you about where I was going. I know I should've told you the truth, and I regret causing you pain. I want you to know I'll never do it again."

Make sure to follow up by telling them how you intend to avoid making the same mistake again. If you aren't sure what they need from you to work on the relationship, you can ask. Just make sure you're ready and willing to actively listen to their answer.

- **Give your partner time**

Even if you're ready to apologize, talk about what happened, and begin working through things, your partner may not feel ready yet. It can take time to come to terms with a betrayal or broken trust.

People process things in different ways, too. Your partner might want to talk right away. But they also might need days or weeks before they can address the issue with you.

It's important to avoid pressuring them to have a discussion before they're ready. Apologize and let your partner know you're ready when they are. If you're struggling in the meantime, consider talking to a counselor who can offer unbiased and supportive guidance.

- **Let their needs guide you**

Your partner may need space and time before they can discuss what happened. And often, this might involve physical space.

This might be difficult to face, but respecting your partner's boundaries and needs can go a long way toward showing them they can depend on you again.

Your partner may want more transparency and communication from you in the future. This is common after a betrayal of trust. You may even willingly share your phone and computer with your partner to prove your honesty.

But if you've made some progress in repairing your relationship and your partner continues to monitor your activities and communications with others, talking to a couple's counselor can help.

- **Commit to clear communication**

In the immediate aftermath of broken trust, you'll want to honestly answer your partner's questions and commit to being completely open with them in the future.

To do this, you have to make sure you're clear on the level of communication they need.

Let's say you broke their trust by withholding some information you didn't think was really important, and you didn't understand why they felt so betrayed. This can indicate there's a deeper issue with communication in your relationship.

If you want to repair your relationship and avoid hurting your partner again in the future, you need to reach a mutual understanding of what good communication looks like.

Miscommunications or misunderstandings can sometimes cause as much pain as intentional dishonesty.

What about the details of an affair?

Relationship counselors often recommend against providing specific details about a sexual encounter with someone else. If you've cheated, your partner may have a lot of questions about what exactly happened. And you might want to answer them in an effort to be transparent.

But talking about the details of an encounter can cause further pain that isn't very productive. If your partner wants details, consider asking them to wait until you can see a therapist together.

The therapist can help you navigate the healthiest way to address these questions. In the meantime, you can still honestly answer their questions without giving explicit details.

- **How long will it take?**

Being in a relationship with broken trust can be extremely uncomfortable. Both sides might be eager to get the whole rebuilding process over with as fast as possible. But realistically, this takes time.

How much time, exactly? It depends on a lot of factors, particularly the event that broke the trust.

Long-standing patterns of infidelity or dishonesty will take longer to resolve. A single lie grounded in a misunderstanding or desire to protect may be easier to address, especially when the partner who lied shows sincere regret and a renewed commitment to communication.

Have patience with yourself. Don't let your partner rush you. A partner who truly regrets hurting you may be hurting, too, but if they truly care for you and want to fix things, they should also understand it isn't helpful to rush right back into the way things were.

- **Is it worth it?**

Rebuilding trust isn't an easy task. It's normal to question if it's even worth it before you decide to commit to working on your relationship.

If your partner makes a mistake or two over the course of a long relationship and owns up to it, working on trust issues may be the right move. As long as there's still love and commitment between the two of you, working on trust issues will only make your relationship stronger.

But if you know you'll never be able to completely trust your partner again, no matter what they do, it's generally best to make this clear right away so you can both begin to move forward separately.

It's also worth weighing your options if you've discovered years of infidelity, financial dishonesty, manipulation, or other major breaches of trust.

Other red flags that might signal it's time to throw in the towel include:

- continued deceit or manipulation
- an insincere apology
- behavior that doesn't match up with their words

- **You don't have to do it alone**

Every relationship goes through a rough patch. There's no shame in reaching out for help.

Couples counseling can be a great resource when dealing with trust issues, particularly those involving infidelity. A counselor can offer an unbiased view of your relationship and help both partners work through underlying issues.

Having tough conversations about betrayal and trust can also bring up painful emotions on both sides. Having a trusted counselor can also help you navigate the difficult feelings as they arise.

- **The bottom line**

It's possible to rebuild a relationship after a breach of trust. Whether it's worth it depends on your relationship needs and whether you feel it's possible to trust your partner again.

If you do decide to try repairing things, be prepared for things to take some time. If both sides are committed to the process of rebuilding trust, you might find that you both come out stronger than before — both as a couple and on your own.

Chapter 4

How to Rescue a Damaged Relationship

You've heard it a million times but it bears repeating: even the strongest relationships face challenges.

Building a happy, healthy partnership takes work and may not always be easy, especially when there's been a breach of trust. "Issues are a part of life and a part of being in a relationship," says clinical psychologist Stone Kraushaar. "And the goal is to not fixate on the past, but work to create together in a meaningful way."

So, how do you go about that? Here are some tips to get you started, whether you're dealing with the fallout from a betrayal or trying to keep a long-distance relationship going.

When there's been a breach of trust

Anytime trust is broken, there's going to be a rift in the relationship. It might be painful to face, but leaving these issues unaddressed won't help anyone in the long run.

1. Take full responsibility if you're at fault

If there has been infidelity or trust has been broken, it's important to take full responsibility for what happened and be understanding of how your behavior hurt your partner.

Avoid becoming defensive or sidestepping your mistake, but don't fall into self-loathing either. "You should own it in a loving way that creates the space to start to rebuild trust," says Kraushaar.

In a nutshell: Take responsibility, but don't attempt to justify your actions or blame them on someone or something else.

2. Give your partner the opportunity to win your trust back

While you have every right to feel hurt and angry, there should be a desire to work on the relationship.

"Trust can never be restored until the person whose trust was broken allows their partner a chance to earn it back,"

3. Practice radical transparency

Instead of bottling up emotions, Kraushaar encourages couples to be "radically transparent" with each other about what has hurt them.

This involves truly getting it all out there, even if you feel a bit silly or self-conscious admitting certain things.

If you're the one who broke the trust, this also involves being radically transparent with yourself about what motivated you to do so. Was it simply a lapse in judgment? Or was it an attempt to sabotage a situation you didn't know how to get out of?

In order to be honest with each other, you'll have to start by being brutally honest to yourselves.

4. Seek professional help

Broken trust can take a toll on everyone in the relationship. If there's been a significant breach, consider working together with a qualified therapist who specializes in relationships and can provide guidance for healing.

5. Extend compassion and care to the person you hurt

If you've hurt your partner, it's easy to fall into a spiral of shame and disappointment in yourself. But that's not going to help either of you. Rather than spend all your time beating yourself up over what you did wrong, try shifting that energy toward showing care and compassion to your partner.

When you're in a long-distance relationship

Being physically apart more often than not can be rough on a relationship. Keeping the romance alive takes extra effort on everyone's part.

1. Manage expectations

Have a discussion with your partner and set ground rules that take into account your exclusiveness and commitment to each other.

Being honest and upfront about your expectations from the beginning can prevent things from going wrong down the road.

2. Have regularly scheduled visits

"It's so important that couples know and have scheduled visits and can look forward to those times and plan to make them special," notes Kraushaar. In fact, research has shown that long-distance relationships where partners have a reunion planned are less stressful and more satisfying.

3. Set aside time for online dates

If you're not able to organize scheduled time together due to significant distance or finances, Kraushaar recommends setting up regular online dates with a theme or specific focus. Don't just go for your usual conversation topics. Cook a meal together, watch a movie while you keep the video chat open, play a virtual game, or even read a short story aloud, taking turns.

4. Don't let your world revolve around your partner

While it's important to pay attention to fostering closeness in a long-distance relationship, that aspect shouldn't consume you.

No matter how much you miss the other person, don't forget about other important areas of your life. Keep up with your hobbies and interests — a happy and healthy relationship partly involves you being each partner being their own person.

When you live together

No matter how you die, going through a rough patch when you live together is stressful.

1. Plan a weekly 'couples meeting'

Kraushaar recommends setting up a specific time each week that allows you both to talk about more difficult topics, such as money, sex, and trust so that these don't bleed over into all of your interactions.

2. Learn to compromise

All relationships require give and take. When you're living in close quarters, being accommodating of the other person's needs and preferences without sacrificing your own can help foster more happiness and fulfillment. Consider working out some kind of temporary agreement that allows each of you to unwind at home alone.

For example, maybe you stay a little later at the gym on Tuesdays and Thursdays, while they hang out with a friend on Mondays and Wednesdays.

3. Spend time with friends outside of your relationship

Spending time with friends can have a powerful effect on your personal mental health and can help strengthen your personal identity. Remember, staying connected to your partner means having a life outside of your relationship.

4. Engage in affectionate physical contact

Kraushaar encourages couples to regularly hug each other in a fully present and connected way. Holding hands or hugging releases oxytocin which can reduce stress and boost your mood.

If you're not on great terms right now, this might be easier said than done. Try starting slow — simply putting your hand on theirs can help to show that you still care.

14. Don't be hooked on romance

Deep-level intimacy is about creating a satisfying and meaningful relationship that isn't always based on romantic expression.

Sure, everyone wants to be swept off their feet from time to time, but it's important to genuinely respect and enjoy your partner for who they are outside of what they can give you.

When you've just had a big fight

Picking up the pieces after a big fight can feel like an impossible task. Try these techniques to help you both move forward.

1. Use skilled communication

Once tempers have calmed down, it's important to make sure you both have a chance to get your points across. Try to give each person space to communicate their point of view.

"Being open and honest about one's thoughts and intentions about the relationship itself and the future can restore — or newly create — a sense of safety" in the relationship

2. Speak from your heart

In order for your partner to truly hear you, it's important to communicate what you're really feeling below all the tension.

For example, avoid accusatory phrases, such as, "You did this to me!" Instead, aim for something along the lines of, "When X happens, I feel Y and I think it would be helpful if you could do Z to reassure me or prevent that from happening in the future."

3. Actively listen

If you catch yourself forming a rebuttal in your head as your significant other is talking, you're not really listening. "You're getting ready to defend yourself or go to battle," says Czajkowska.

"Winning" an argument is never truly winning, she adds. "If your partner feels that they lost, it will likely contribute to more distance, tension, and resentment, so in the long run, you lose too."

4. Break the pattern

When rebuilding the relationship, Czajkowska advises to consider it a new one, rather than saving an old one.

"Seeing it this way creates an opportunity for defining rules and boundaries from the beginning." This means striving to understand and work through underlying issues as well as letting go of past resentments you've been holding onto.

When you just aren't feeling it

A lack of passion or case of the "mess" doesn't automatically mean your relationship is beyond repair.

1. Look at the upside of your relationship

Spend a week noticing or writing down all the things your partner does "right."

Researchers have found that we tend to see what we are looking for. If you're looking for reasons to be mad or upset with your partner, you'll probably find them. But this works in reverse, too. Keep your eyes peeled for the good things."

2. Say 'thank you' for the small things

Similarly, don't just silently observe your partner's right-doings. When they do something that's kind of helpful, even if it's just tidying up the kitchen after a meal, verbally thank them.

3. Have fun together

Sometimes, you just fall into a rut. It might sound cliche, but setting aside some time, even just a few hours, to go do something out of the ordinary can make a big difference.

Psychological research shows that partners who play together experience more positive emotions and report greater happiness.

Try taking a break from the same old routine and spend time participating in novel, uplifting experiences.

keep the spark

Here are a few ideas to get you started:
- Take a one-time class together.
- Grab a deck of cards or a board game you both used to love and head to the park.

- Scan your local weekly paper for unusual events. Even if you're not totally sure what the event entails, make a plan to go check it out together, whether it's a craft fair or a car show.

1. Maintain intimacy and communication

Establish how to take care of each other emotionally.

What does this actually mean? For starters, commit to giving each other a heads up when it feels like you're drifting apart. Sit down together and look at what might be causing that. Have you both been wrapped up in work? Has it been too long since you spent the day just enjoying each other's company?

"Commitment to working on the relationship is just as important as commitment to the partner," she emphasizes.

Is it worth it?

There's no easy answer here. Ultimately, you'll need to evaluate whether the relationship is worth the work that's required to save it from a low point.

It's also wise to make sure everyone involved is committed to saving the relationship. If you're the only one willing to put in the work, reconciliation probably isn't likely. That said, abuse of any kind, whether it's physical, verbal, or emotional, is a red flag. Keep in mind that signs of toxicity can be quite subtle. Are you walking on eggshells around your partner? Have you lost your confidence or sense of self?

Printed in Great Britain
by Amazon